When J ... she spea ... who love Him.

Dear God...
You amaze me!

You enter my mind
In tiny sunbeams of thought
Enlightening
Lifting
Putting me at peace...
So that suddenly
From *within* my
Eyes see clearly.
As clearly as tho the
Curtains had been parted
Or the underbrush pulled away
From in front of a cave...

And I walk out
Singing softly.

"...inspiration for your own quiet time through touching, thoughtful...prayers."

Florence Littauer, author of *Personality Plus*

You Bring the Umbrellas, LORD

Joy Morgan Davis

Fleming H. Revell
A Division of Baker Book House Co
Grand Rapids, Michigan 49516

Library of Congress Cataloging-in-Publication Data

Davis, Joy Morgan.
    You bring the umbrellas, Lord / Joy Morgan Davis.
       p.   cm.
    ISBN 0-8007-5421-2
    1. Christian poetry, American.   I. Title.
  PS3554.A9349126Y68   1992
811'.54—dc20   91-41758
                                             CIP

Copyright © 1992 by Joy Morgan Davis
Published by Fleming H. Revell
a division of Baker Book House Company
P.O. Box 6287, Grand Rapids, MI 49516-6287

ISBN: 0-8007-5421-2

Fifth printing, May 1994

Printed in the United States of America

This book is for . . .

Becky,
   Whose gift of poetry
   Gave me the idea.

Carolyn,
   Who said I could
        And said I could
             And said I could
   Until I believed
   I could.

Mary,
   Who said nothing,
   But prayed.

Contents

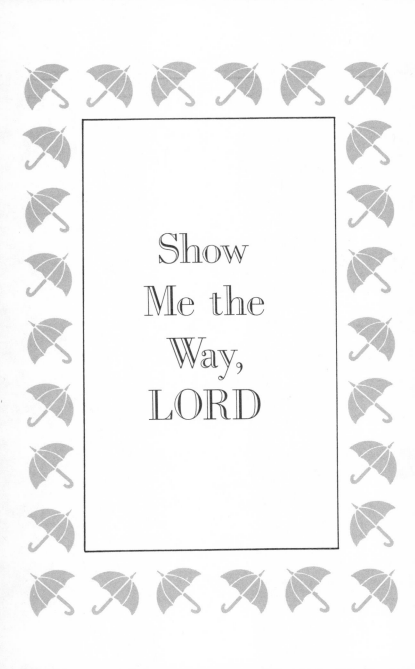

Show Me the Way, LORD

Covered

Just now You said,
"Proceed!"

But I've been waiting
Until I saw a
Clear blue sky,
Wanting to know
The weather report
Before I went . . .

I've known all along
It was Your will,
That it was You
Who gave me the mind
For this adventurous
Venture,
But there was such
Uncertainty . . .
Will it rain, storm,
Hail, high water?

"Maybe. Proceed!"

Oh, good!
I've wanted to go . . .
Now I can!
You bring the
Umbrellas, Lord!

The Song

Dear God . . .
You amaze me!

You enter my mind
In tiny sunbeams of thought
Enlightening
Lifting
Putting me at peace . . .
So that suddenly
From *within*, my
Eyes see clearly,
As clearly as tho the
Curtains had been parted
Or the underbrush pulled away
From in front of a cave . . .

And I walk out,
Singing softly.

Static

I left messages,
Lord, but You didn't
Get back to me!
(And I *told* You it
Was urgent!)
Are You away on
Business?
Is there plague or pestilence
Somewhere more important
Than me?

"Dear child, I *tried*
To call, but your line
Was busy.
Stop talking and listen
For My voice."

Walk This Way

You must think me foolish,
Lord, or at the very least
Forgetful.
You tell me time and time
Again that You are
Walking with me,
Holding back the branches,
Preceding, weeding,
Making the way.

But when I'm faced with
A tangled forest
I need to see
The path.

Could You make it
Clearer, Lord,
One more time?

Opening Night

Dear Lord,
There looms on my horizon
The promise of a
Problem . . .
Not a little problem,
A large one,
And very invasive.
As You know,
I pray
It won't develop,
But if it should
(As seems so certain)
It will be a life-altering
Time.
After practicing my faith
For half a century
This may be the time I've been
Practicing *for!*

I trust I've learned
My lessons well . . .
That when the time comes
I can stand with that rare
Courage portrayed by other disciples
In other times of testing.
I trust I will be strong.
I want to be
A worthy witness.
I want to
Perform with *practiced*
Grace!

Prepare me, Lord.
Teach me my lines . . .
Show me my entrances
And exits . . .
And help me not to have
Stage fright.

Mapmaker

Thank You, Lord,
That the decision
Does not have to be made
Tonight,
For tonight I have
No answers . . .
I don't know
What to do,
Or which way
To go!
But I know You and I
Will continue to talk
About it . . .
Day by day,
Step by step,
Until it's time to
Take a direction
One way or another . . .
And by then, I'm sure,
It will seem as if
There is only one road
In front of me—
The right road!

Meanwhile
I'll just wait . . .
While You draw the
Map!

Transformation

O Lord,
It was such a little thing . . .
Someone said,
"You mean so much
To me!"

And suddenly my empty heart
Was filled . . .
Love
Joy
Grace
Mercy—
A cornucopia overflowing with
Fruits of the Spirit!

Such a little thing,
Lord! A single sentence . . .
Yet it turned my meager fare
Into Thanksgiving's feast!

This Is the Day

Dear Lord, In this day
That You have made
Help me not to be
Afraid of joy!
Just now my life is filled
To overflowing
With beauty and abundance,
Yet I am too timid
To touch it!
I walk warily
Around it . . .
As if seeing suddenly a
Rare piece of priceless crystal
Sparkling in the sunlight . . .
Will it break?

Is it mine to keep,
Or must I give it back?
Is it just to look at,
Or is it here
To have and to hold?
Help me to be bold . . .
Bold enough to believe it,
To take it to me,
To embrace it.
O Dear Lord,
Tomorrow my assignment
May be sorrow,
But today
It is happiness . . .

I will rejoice
And be glad
In it!

Light of My Life

Yesterday I couldn't even
See my way, much less the end
Of the tunnel.
Today I still can't see
The end, but the *lights* have
Come on!
Many lights, in a
Multitude of
Colors!

O Dear God, thank You!
It's still a tunnel . . .
But now it's technicolored!

Old Business

Just now a long-forgotten book
Fell open, and I found
Between the pages
A List . . .
All my prayers
And problems!
An earnest, lengthy list it was,
Of needs and sadnesses,
But long-forgotten, like the book,
For those were prayers
Of years ago . . .
And *answered* years ago!

So! Just now
As I sat praying,
Pouring out the problems
That so pressed
My heart until it hurt,
I read again
The List . . .
No longer necessary,
Gone, forgotten, forgiven,
Each matter now dismissed!

And I thought . . .
Thank God. This too
Shall pass!

Breakthrough

It never ceases to amaze me, Lord . . .
That moment when my plane
Breaks through the darkening clouds
Into the clear, bright blue
Expanse of space
Which we call "sky."
Today it took
My breath away!
There was this
Ceiling of uncertainty . . .
Dense, low, and restless,
Disturbed by unseen storms . . .
But as the silver arrow rose
And pierced the raging
Billows, they proved to be
No barrier!
The fear was superficial,
For we were so soon
Free!

Lord, help me to remember
That moment . . .
The feel of flight
Soaring through uncertainty . . .
As through my clouds of fear and doubt
And dark foreboding
I send my silver arrows . . .
Faith
     Hope
          Trust
               Truth . . .
Until I'm free!

Nightlight

Lord, this is not
A good night.
I'm sick,
And sad,
And sorry for myself.
Despite Your constant blessings
I'm close to despair.
Why am I so weak
Of spirit
As well as of body?
Why . . .
When I know You
Are always
Faithful?

Help me to remember
The many mornings
I have seen Your new mercies . . .
And that dawn is now only
Six hours away.

God's Specialty

There are some things
Too big to say in
A sentence, Lord,
Like the Miracle
You made for me
Today!
It would take
A page just to tell
How I got *into* this mess,
And a page . . . no!
A *book* of pages to tell
How You got me out.
I am astonished!
I want to stand
And tell the whole
World how overwhelmed
I am . . . but there are
Not enough words.

You said it all, Lord,
When You said . . .
"All things are possible."

The Long, Long Trail

O Lord,
I try so
Continually
To get where I'm going . . .
But often I drive my wagon
Into the brambles!
I frequently fight my way
Through the tangled underbrush
Instead of finding
Your path . . .
And even when I arrive at
The right destination,
I'm all scratched
And bruised and bleeding,
Having struggled through thorns
That You never intended.

I try so hard, Lord,
To cross the rivers
Without sinking,
To climb the mountains
Without fainting,
To walk the valleys
Without fear.
I *try!*
It's my best attribute . . .
And my worst.

Help me to release,
To listen,
To let go of the reins . . .
And just ride
Beside You!

Apprentice

It's almost tomorrow,
And tomorrow is
So important, Lord.
When I meet my friend
There will be fences to mend
In our relationship . . .
In fact, there are
All *sorts* of things
To be repaired . . .
And I know so little
Of carpentry.

Can You teach me . . .
Tonight?

Private Lessons

There's so much in my life
That seems hard just now . . .
The days are long,
The nights even longer . . .
My body aches
Persistently,
My mind thinks
Melancholy thoughts,
And my spirit, Lord,
My spirit is low.
Lately I've endured
Misunderstanding,
Made mistakes,
Wrestled with heartache
And hurt . . .
All at once.

Help me to remember
That faith is not a feeling
But a fact,
That Your care is consistent . . .
Help me to live the Christian
Philosophy of life
I so easily teach . . .

Oh, today, Lord,
It is I who needs
To be taught.

To God Be the Glory

O Lord!
I look at my life . . .
The life into which You have
Poured peace and faith
And fulfillment . . .
And I see
I would have been
Literally *lost*
Without You!

When there was trouble
You intervened,
When there was trial
You were with me,
When my heart broke
You mended it,

When I wondered
Which way to go
At countless crossroads
You turned me
Each time in the
Right direction.

Indeed, whenever I hurt,
Or failed,
Or faced confusion,
The only thing *I* ever did
Was come to You
For help.

Mercy! It seems
My only merit is that
When there's an
Emergency
I know who to call!

LORD,
Let Me
Remind
You

Request at Dawn

Good morning, Lord!
May I remind You, please,
That my husband needs
A small miracle today?
Not a very large miracle,
You understand . . .
You don't need to move
A mountain, or part the sea,
Or stop forty days of downpour,
Or even multiply the
Loaves and fishes . . .
Nothing so much as all that!
Just something purely personal,
From You, to him!

You see, he's
Been beset and besieged
On all sides lately
As he copes with the
Corporate world.
He's a brave man, Lord,
Constant and true,
And like all
Knights in shining armor

He's fought the dragons
Long and hard.
But last night he said,
With a whispered sigh,
That his sword seemed dull
And his armor heavy.

So . . . Is there some small
Miracle You could send down
Today? Something, well,
Wonderful! Just to let him
Know You're there.
(It's still morning, and You have
Plenty of time!)

"Yes, the day is just dawning,
And I know all
About your Knight.
Let Me love him!
It's what I do best.
For My love *is* a
Miracle . . . a miracle of the heart
Waiting to happen.
You'll see!"

Good evening, Lord!
I did! I surely did
See!

37

The Cave

The entrance to the cave
Was steep, and deep,
And dark.
I ascended, having seen the
Centuries-old stalagmites
Mirrored in a crystal lake
So still and undisturbed.

In the sunlight stood a child
Of the British Isles . . .
Her skin
As pure as porcelain,
Her eyes
As blue as the Bermuda sea,
Her words
Were clipped Queen's English,
"Is it very frightening
Down there then?"

I laughed
And leaned low.
"Oh no! It's beautiful!
So many colors and a
Crystal lake you'll love!"

Lord, I'm standing here
Looking down now.
The way seems
Dark and steep and deep today.
You're the Guide!
You lead the way . . .

But before we go
Tell me it's beautiful.

Dividends

The financial graph
Showed the ups and downs
And levels of my
Capital accumulation . . .
"You see," said the counselor,
"How you had the greatest growth
During periods of national
Peace and prosperity,
When the economic climate
Was favorable."

Fascinating.

On my *spiritual* graph the growth
Always appears during periods of
Trial,
Trouble,
Disappointment and pain,
When the climate is
Anything but favorable.

Indeed, Lord . . .
It seems I have invested
In adversity!

Precious Lord, Take My Hand . . .

Thank You, Lord,
For this time of enforced
Trust . . .
This time of trial
When I must keep
Reminding me of You.
I always love You, Lord,
I always listen . . .
But only when the fog
Is this thick
Do I hold Your hand
So tightly.

Nearly There

We've walked so far
Together, Lord . . .
From the cold, clear silent waters
Of that country creek
Where a trusting, true little girl
Was baptized,
To this roaring metropolis
That teems with a
Million or more souls,
We've walked . . .
For fifty years!

I remember bright meadows, and
Valleys, some shadowed and deep, and
Rivers rushing dangerously
Toward the falls, and
Mountains to climb
(Where You pushed and pulled),
And peaks of joy and praise and
Accomplishment, and
Plateaus of sameness,
Time and again and again.

Sometimes You carried me.
Sometimes we walked side by side.

Sometimes I ran along
Ahead of You, but You never let me
Out of Your sight.

It's been a good walk,
Lord . . . a good walk.
But I tire so much more easily now.
Even in my sensible shoes
I tire,
And I look forward to
The time when we can rest.

We've walked so far
Together, Lord,
That we're closer to
Your house than to mine.
Take me home with You . . .
Now! Tonight! I'm ready!

And if not tonight, then
Soon! Before I have to buy
Another pair of
Sensible shoes . . .

Or crutches.

Or a cane.

The Cross

Aren't You tired of my
Tears, Lord?
I've been sad for
So long
About this same situation . . .
If You could just see
Your way clear to
Resolve it . . . soon, maybe?
We could move on to
Something else,
You and I.

What's that You say, Lord?
When it's time?
When the lesson is
Learned . . . the bridge
Built . . . the plan
Completed?
I have to wait till *then*,
Lord?

Ah, well. Whatever draws
Me nearer.

Sudden Insight

My prayers, lately,
Have been rather
Pointed, Lord . . .
About this need
Of mine.
You know it's real,
You know why,
And You must know
When You'll answer . . .
But You haven't yet
Made a move!

Maybe I should quit
Asking for action
And pray for patience.

Soul Mate

It is midnight . . .
Dark, outside and in,
And at this moment
I wonder, fretfully, forgetfully,
Was there ever anyone else
Who felt so lost, so alone,
So forsaken,
So desperate in the night
To know His will
To find His peace
To feel His favor
Once again.

David . . .
King
Conqueror
Deceiver
Sinner
A man after God's own heart . . .
What an overwhelming mixture of
Strength and faith
And wanton weaknesses.
Yet, when the battle cries
Died, and the crowds
Were gone away,
When David wandered alone

Through the silent, secret hills
Of his heart
He wept,
As I weep,
To know God's peace
To feel His forgiveness
To see His face . . .
For David could not bear
To be without Him . . .

And from such anguish of the soul
There poured those precious songs,
Those everlasting, loving songs,
Of praise
Of grace and forgiveness
Of refuge
And a very present help in
Time of trouble . . .
Music for the midnight hours.

And I read them now . . .
Soul searching,
Grasping the promises as
I would grasp a lifeline,
Seeking
Accepting
Singing . . .

King David and I,
At midnight.

To Be Like Him

O Dear Lord Jesus,
Why is it that my moments
Of greatest creativity
Come during my times of
Greatest grief? It's a terrible
Price to pay!

"Yes, it was . . .
For Me too."

48

Spectacle

Lord, do You remember
That day in Dothan
When the King of Syria
Sent his army to march
Upon the city
And seize Your man Elisha?
It must have seemed
A frightful sight . . . to see
An army marching
Toward the gates!

But Elisha's eyes were open,
Truly open,
To see beyond the enemy.
He saw Your heavenly hosts . . .
The horses and
The chariots of fire . . .
Surrounding him, sealing him,
In flaming circles
Of safety!

O Lord, when the armies
March against *my* gates,
(And they will) . . .
Please, Sir,
Let me see
The chariots!

Fragrance at My Feet

For so long, Lord,
I've lived with a
Beloved dream . . .
My dearest and best
Dream!
I believed it so trustingly
It seemed already
True,
And I waited only for
The time to come when
I could claim it!

There came instead the time
When I knew I never could . . .
Never. The dream was never
Coming true.
And in my soul there was
A sound, a shattering
Of this precious thing
For so long, so dear to me.

That was today, Lord, today.
My best, beloved dream
Lies all around my feet
In pieces,
So many pieces I can't
Pick them up.
I've prayed . . .
You've promised . . .
I have at my disposal
All the King's horses
And all the King's men . . .
But it can't be put
Together again.
It can't.
O Lord, what good are
Broken dreams?

"You say it can't be put
Together again?
Neither could the
Alabaster box.
But oh, what fragrance
Filled the air, as Mary
Wiped away her tears!"

I Lay Me Down . . .

I'm so excited about
Tomorrow, Lord,
I can't sleep tonight,
And I need to sleep . . .
Tomorrow will be
So wonderful
I don't want to be
Tired.

Would You now just
Settle my mind and
Soothe my nerves . . .
And help me to store
My "strength for the day"
Tonight?

Spelling Bee

I'm remembering,
Lord,
How my mother taught
Your Word to a
Large class of ladies,
The J.O.Y. Class . . .
Jesus first
Others second
Yourself last!

Spelled correctly
That's the formula for
A lifetime of service
And satisfaction!

O Lord,
When I write
My name,
Help me not to
Get it backward!

Be Still My Soul

You have performed
Many miracles
In my life, Lord, especially
During these last few days.
What I had thought would be rough
Has been smooth,
What I had thought would be narrow
Has been wide,
And what I had feared
Would cause my collapse
Has become, instead,
My foundation!

How I dreaded the yoke
And rebelled at the burden . . .
But lo! The yoke is easy
And the burden is light . . .
And once more You have proved
That the impossible
CAN BE!

When will I learn that
Whatever You choose,
Wherever You lead,
There, and there only is my peace
And my prosperity?
When will my soul
Simply rest . . .
And wait upon Thee?

Perspective

The disappointment was
So deep I felt
I'd never, ever
Be the same.
I felt abandoned,
Left alone!
"Lord," I whispered,
"Where *were* You?
Where was Your
Mighty Hand . . .
When all it would have
Taken would have been
A touch . . .
A single touch to give me
What I wanted, needed,
Hoped and wished for . . .
Why did You leave me
Without help?"

But life went on,
Despite despair,
And I was bound to it . . .
Bound to learn to live
With it,
Bound to make some meaning
Out of it,
Bound to be better
Because of it . . .
And finally I was forced
To come so close
To Him
That I could
View it from His
Vantage point!
I saw the whole
Of it! And seeing, knew,
I had not been abandoned . . .

I had been blessed.

O LORD, This Is a Rugged Way

Walk With a King

O Lord, this is a rugged way
   That leaves me weak and worn . . .
By rocks my hands and feet are bruised,
   By tangled thickets torn!
Why would this clogged and clouded path
   Become Your choice for me?
Why not the higher, wider way
   Where visions I could see?

"Oh Child, it is enough to know
   I cherish all My own . . .
And that this is the only road
   That leads you to My throne!
But through the valleys of travail,
   Through long and lonely days
I'll not forget I gave My word
   To walk with you always!"

Then lift me, Lord . . . I'll lean on You!
   We'll travel on as one!
Your mighty hand will hold me up
   Until the journey's done!
Meanwhile my quiet, unquestioning soul
   Won't ask You to explain . . .
I know Your rugged way is best,
   Because I know You reign!

Casting All Care

Dear God, do You hear me
   When nightly I weep . . .
When through the dark hours
   My vigil I keep?
I wonder if You know
   I'm weary and worn . . .
If You sense I'm feeling
   So lost and forlorn?
I need You to answer,
   To show me the light . . .
To whisper Your wisdom,
   And tell me what's right!

"My Child, I am listening,
   I hear your request . . .
I know what you need, and
   Your heart will be blest.
I know about burdens,
   I carried the cross . . .
Now trust Me to carry
   Your sadness and loss!
So put away worry,
   Tonight you will sleep.
Just rest with assurance . . .
   My *promise* I'll *keep!*"

Beauty for Ashes

Dear Lord, I dreamed of how it would be . . .
   To love so gloriously!
I dreamed of how I would always live . . .
   And walk victoriously!
But dreams can die or disappear,
   And hopes can fall apart,
When all seems lost and I am left
   With only a broken heart.

"My Child, I know how your heart must break,
   Whenever a dream you lose . . .
But let Me reshape it to be at last
   A vessel that I can use!
I'll give you beauty for ashes of dust,
   I'll give you a song in the night . . .
And soon you will see that your broken dreams
   Have led you to live in My light!"

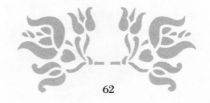

Something to Love

Lord, surely there must be a task for me,
    Something of service to You.
I want to do great and glorious things,
    But one small assignment will do.
I've trusted Your will and Your way for me,
    So now let my life be a part
Of all the miraculous things I've seen
    Since You have come into my heart!
You might have a mountain for me to move,
    Or one little race to be run.
You might need a mission for all the world,
    Or one little deed to be done.
Perhaps You will want me to whisper a word
    To someone whose soul is in need,
Or maybe You'll send me to harvest Your fields,
    Or give me Your lambs to feed.

Whatever it is, I will wait for Your time,
    To teach me which gift to give . . .
But let me have *something* to love for You,
    For then I shall truly live!

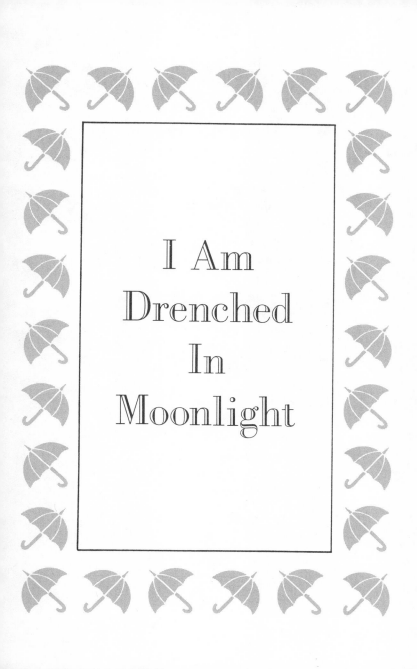

I Am
Drenched
In
Moonlight

Where Are the Treasures?

I am drenched
In moonlight.
I would drink it
If I could . . .
This soft, silvery
Liquid light that pours
Over my body
Washing away the lines of
Weariness and worry
Until I am
Fresh, free, glowing
From my bath.

And I wonder . . .

Would I truly *know*
This tranquil night
If my day had not been
So troubled?

Would peace be peace
If peace was all
There was?
And what of joy?
Is joy more precious
After sorrow, and if so,
Should I ask for sorrow
So I may know joy?
Where is the treasure?
In the light?
Or in the darkness
That makes me know
The light?

I am not sure.
So I shall accept them both
As gifts from God,
Grateful . . .

While I bathe in moonlight.

One to a Family

I am *really* tired of continually
Trying to make everything
Right . . .
To placate and accommodate.
If nobody *else* cares
Whether we have meals together
Or if vacations are
Pleasant
Or if we make it to the pageant
On Independence Day . . .
Who am I
To rearrange their lives?

If two of them, or three of them,
Or all of them

Want to declare war
And scream and cry
Or not speak at all
Or lock doors and not
Let each other in . . .
Who am I
To suggest peace?

If hearts are broken
And plans destroyed
And youthful dreams are
Dashed against the
Hard unyielding rocks of reality
And scattered in a million and one ways
Who am I
To pick up the pieces?
Who am I?

Mother.

My Son, the Graduate

Go West, Young Man,
Go West . . .
Like Duke Wayne you will
Sit tall in the saddle as you
Ride to take the sunset.
Success is yours, and we
Send you to it . . .
Bravely, brightly, with
Rightly arranged smiles on our
Faces, looking at you
With the love and logic
That tells us you are
Wise and wonderful
And grown in grace
And ready, oh yes,
Ready!
And so you go,
Galloping toward life
As we stand waving wildly,
Shouting our good-byes . . .

While hid behind my heart
There is the sad, insistent
Whisper . . .
Come back, young man,
Come back.

Facade

There is a mirage
In my mirror . . .
The forever-young face
So delicately done in
Soft colors and creams
That cover the
Always advancing conquest
Of age!
I am lulled into
A fond forgetfulness . . .
Until I notice,
As I write,
My mother's hand
Holding the pen.

Let Me Count the Ways

How much do I love you?
Well, let me see . . .
I love you when I wake up
In the morning
And when I go to sleep
At night . . .
And in between!

I love the way you look
In the sunlight,
With your auburn hair
And amber eyes.

I love you when we are
Laughing and lighthearted . . .
When we work, and play,
And stay . . .
And are still together through
Thick and thin.

I love you,
Oh, how I love you when you
Take the children in your arms
And hold them tight . . .
Protecting, teaching,
Giving them the gift of
Assurance and self-worth.

I love you standing stoic
In the storm . . .
Waiting, hoping, praying,
Calm,
Until tomorrow comes.

I love you,
With all my heart,
As long as we both shall live.
And then,
After that, my Darling,
You will be
My dearest friend . . .

Forever.

Good Thinking!

I forgot my gloves
One windy, wintery day.
"If your hands get cold
I'll hold them," my husband said
And he did.

I'm thinking of
Throwing away all
My gloves!

Surprise

I remember
Vividly
That day in third grade
When I realized (with a start)
That I was not the prettiest, smartest,
Cutest little girl
In class.

Mercy!
Mother was wrong!

Old Flames

Wistfully I watched
The youthful pair . . .
Their hands clasped, so close,
Their love as shining,
As radiant as the sun!
Misty-eyed I turned,
Remembering a time
My love had touched
Me so . . .
A time when toward the sun
We ran together,
Leaping in the light!

But that was then,
And now the shadows lengthen . . .

We walk sedately
Through the twilight time
Of life,
Too peaceful for the fiery
Passions of such joy or sorrow
Or possession,
Too comfortably content
To be consumed.
We are so settled in the shade,
Perhaps the sun
Would hurt our eyes . . .
And yet,
I wonder.

I wonder also . . .
Does *he* wonder?
Is he wistful too?

A Woman's View

Men are marvelous when
It comes to
Conquering the world!
They put out fires,
Lead revolutions,
Move mountains and rivers
With their machines,
And rescue
Kittens from trees.
If a problem requires
Action they act . . .
Stoic, stouthearted,
The solution so simple,
To men.

But there are some things
That can't be fixed
With hammers and nails
And sandbags . . .
Like the flood of tears already wasted
Which can't be gotten back again

Or broken hearts
Or long lost dreams
Or love that hurts or
Silence
When words were needed.
There are some things that are
Always going to be wrong, not right,
And have to be endured,
Day by day by day by day
By day.

And men . . . when faced with the
Frustration of a brick wall
Are anxious to the point of
Anger. Robbed of action, they can only
Rant and rave as to what
Should be done, and what *could* be
Done, and where, and why, and when!

Oh . . . how I wish he would stop,
Just *stop* . . . and touch me
Tenderly.

Special

There are others who
Have walked with me
Through times of love
Or celebration, or weariness
Or woe . . .

But only you left lasting
Footprints on my life,
Forever to remind me
Of our paths.

I Thee Endow

If I had treasures
I would lay them at your feet
And pave your path with
Golden coins.

Instead I've made a
Carpet of my dreams . . .

Tread softly,
Love.

Landscapes

There are twenty years
Between the two . . .
My child
And my child's child!
Twenty years between two children
Who are the dear
Delight of my life
My pleasure
My treasure
My love . . .
Each child the same!

But in *me* a miracle occurred . . .
A metamorphosis!
I am no longer "Mother"
With a thousand things to
Sort . . .
With hurried, worried,
Weary days and nights . . .

Sometimes losing sight of love
In the avalanche of
Meals
Manners
Measles
Costumes for the Christmas pageant
And sudden adolescence . . .
I am "Grandmother"!

I hug without hurry.
I talk. She listens.
I spin old-time tales
Like long threads linking
Our lives
Generation to generation.
I rest.
The large, looming mountain
Of responsibility is moved . . .

And I can see the scenery
Of love!

What Are Friends For?

The experience had left me
Wounded, weeping . . .
And I poured out my
Sad account of the false
Accusation, the hurt,
The humiliation
That was so unfair.

She listened with her
Whole heart,
As I had known
She would,
And then she said softly,
"When you cry
I taste the salt."

Once more she'd
Shared my soul.
I was not surprised . . .
We're friends.

Echoes

I can hear the harmony
Even now . . .
The old treadmill sewing machine
Humming along
As she sang to herself . . .
"Jesus is near
To comfort and cheer
Just when I need Him
Most. . . ."
And as a child
I would wonder if He
Was standing right beside her!

Now I know . . .
For I too have found Him there,
His hand on my shoulder,
And so will
My own daughter,
    And her daughter,
        And her daughter . . .

Faith of our
Mothers . . .
Living faith!

God's Child

At ten years her
Tiny shoulders were too small
To bear the burdens
Of the world,
But she tried . . .

When Angela and Amy
Refused to play
The game together she
Pulled them from their
Separate sides of the room . . .
"Please kiss and make up,"
She pleaded.

When William spilled
His finger paints and
Left the table in a temper
She followed him . . .
"At least you made
A picture,"
She soothed.

When it rained on
Picnic Day and the
Class sat gloomily
Inside with their sandwiches
She walked to the window . . .
"But the *flowers* look
Delighted," she observed.

I watched,
Remembering . . .
Blessed are the Peacemakers
For they shall be called
The children of God.

Keep
Reminding
Me,
LORD

Garden of Prayer

Keep reminding me, Lord!
Keep saying, "I love you,
I will lead you,
I will keep you
Close,
I care," . . . for I need so
To hear it.

That's why I come
To the garden
Alone . . .
And listening.

The Shepherd

Lord . . .

Don't let me wonder, worrisome, about
The future . . . where? when? how?
Haven't You always taken
Care of me,
Led, loved me, lighted
The way?

I trust.

Reflection in the Rain

Is it all right if I
Cry, Lord?
I'm despondent,
Near despair,
My mood is
Deep, deep blue.

It's not that I don't
Trust You . . .
I do!
It's not that I don't
Know Your plan
Is best . . .
I do!
I'm sure that tomorrow,

Or next week
Or next year
I'll see that this day
Doesn't matter . . .
You will have either
Erased the deep, deep blue
Or blended it with
Other colors to make
A rainbow . . .
I know that!

But right now I can't
Keep the tears from falling
Like rain around me.
Why, I wonder?

"O Child, a simple truth . . .
The rain must make a
Mirror
For My rainbow!"

Compensation

I don't like it, Lord,
That my body becomes
More cranky and decrepit
Every day . . .
But I like it that
I've acquired
Some new senses . . .

I see now
With my soul,
I feel now
With my heart,
I hear now
With understanding . . .
And I know the composure
And calm
That comes only
With age.

Thank You, Lord,
For large
Favors!

Moving Day

Will I lose her, Lord, if she moves
Away . . . outside the city to those
Acres and acres of lonesome land,
Away from all we've shared as
Friends . . . will I lose her?

Will the friendship be infrequent
So that finally we know so
Little of each other's lives we feel
Removed, remote?
Will we become "acquaintances"?

I can't imagine it. I miss her
Already. Who will I
Talk to, cry to, listen to,
Pray with, love as
I love her?
Will the laughter between us be
Silent?
Will the games we've played be played
Ever again?

I don't know . . .
I just know I need her.
Don't let her move, Lord,
At least
Not out of my life.

Tell Me the Time

What time *is* it,
Lord?
I know Your Word says
There's a time for
Everything
Under the sun . . .
A time to be born, a time
To die,
A time to sow, a time
To reap,
A time to laugh, a time
To cry . . .
But often I'm not sure
Which
I should do
When!

Should I stand stoic,
Enduring the status quo,
Or should I try to move
Heaven and earth to
Change things?
Should I speak my mind
Or hold my tongue?
Should I march righteously
Into the Red Sea,
Or should I use the good sense
You gave me and stay high,
Dry, sensible, and safe?

It's such a dilemma, Lord!
I'm listening . . .
Just tell me the time!

Without Doubt

I know
If I have faith,
Dear Lord,
I'm not supposed
To have fear.
But I feel so weak
This morning . . .
I'm afraid in spite
Of myself.

"Dear Child,
It doesn't matter
How you feel . . .
It only matters
That I AM
Still faithful."

Saints Alive!

You've said, Lord,
That precious in Your sight
Is the death of Your
Saints . . .
And since I'm
One of them,
I know that even now
You are eagerly
Waiting,
Watching,
Joyously counting the days
Until I come
To live with You!

So, Lord,
Since You are
Counting the days,
I want so much to make
Every day count . . .

Joyously!

My Mistake, Lord

Why is it, Lord . . .
When You answer my prayers
I always think . . .
This is too good to be
True?
Isn't this what I've begged
You for on bended knee,
Tearfully telling You
What You already knew,
Reminding You
Time after time
Of my need?

Now it has all
Come to pass!
Complete!
More than I imagined . . .
Abundantly more than
I believed . . .
And still I wake up wondering,
How could I have been
So "lucky"?
O Lord, You must be sadly
Amazed at my lack
Of insight . . .
When I mistake
A Miracle
For a Four-Leaf Clover!

Colorfast

The stark, stiff branches of the
Bare old trees were
Thin and brittle
Like an old man's bones
As they stretched up and out,
Gray on gray on gray,
To streak the winter landscape
And the sky . . .
And I could hear
The crunch of crackling snow
Beneath my feet
As I trudged heavily
Across the frozen field toward
The hunter's pond
Behind the pasture.

Then! Coming on it suddenly
I caught my breath!
A tall magnolia . . .

The snow still packed
Around its roots
The ice still caked
Along its limbs . . .
But the leaves,
Those lovely leaves
Were green, bright green,
Like satin with a sheen . . .
And I stood still,
Barely breathing, absorbing the
Sudden unexpected color
In the cold!

Dear Lord! When I walk at last
Into the winter of my life,
With brittle bones
And my branches bent,
How glorious to know
My soul is
Evergreen!

Battlefield

Today,
Dear Lord,
I feel like Paul
The apostle . . .
At his worst.
What I do,
I would not . . .
And what I would,
I do not!
Like Paul,
I seem to be
Constantly caught
Between
My earthly deeds and
My heavenly desires!
It's like a war
Inside me . . .
How can I win?

"Surrender."

Search

We're flying through cloudy skies
Today, Lord.

It was gloomy even when we
Left the ground,
And now that we
Are airborne
There's nothing else on either side
Except masses of great,
Gray, cumulus clouds
Like so much wool . . .
Dark wool.
The pilot keeps flying
Up, Up, Up . . .
Looking for
The sun.

I was thinking just
This morning, Lord . . .
My *life* has been a little
Gloomy lately.

Keep me looking up . . .
Until I see
The Son.

The Theater

Lord,
We know so little of life,
The *whole* of life . . .
For we are like the actor who moves
Across the stage
From wing to wing
Playing only his own part
Saying only his own lines . . .
Not knowing how they will fit
Into the finished play.

But when at last
You lift the curtain
On that Grand Performance
We shall see it through from
Beginning to End.

We shall see the
Sense of it,
And we will be glad that
We were there . . .
To hear our call
To take our cue
When it was our time to be
On stage!

So, Lord, I'll say the words
To the best of my ability,
And stand in my
Appointed place!
I don't need to know the plot . . .

I know the Playwright!

Just You and Me, Lord

I'm so lonesome, Lord!
It's a beautiful day . . .
The grass is green from
Spring rains,
The sky is a clean, clear
Blue,
And the lake
Reflects its light . . .
But I want to be with someone
Who loves me,
Who understands my thoughts,
Who knows my dreams,
Who shares my soul search
For joy, peace, faith,
Fulfillment!

My husband loves me,
But he is away
Conquering the world.
My children love me,
But they have
Lives, loves,
Children of their own . . .

My dearest and best
Companions love me,
But they are busy being
Companions to other people
Lately . . .
So I'm lonesome, really
Lonesome!

I almost asked You, just now,
If You knew about that,
About being alone . . .
But then I remembered that You
Were the loneliest Man on earth,
That there was literally not
Another person like You
In all the world.
You *must* know all about it,
How to manage it,
What to make of it!

So, Lord,
Could we be alone
Together?

Sixth Sense

Indeed, Dear Lord,
I see through a glass darkly.

The drape of Time and Eternity
Is drawn so close across
The windows of this world
That I cannot see beyond
Into that other World,
Where angels rise and sing
While ransomed souls
Surround the Throne of Grace . . .
So close I cannot know
Or understand the things on earth
That seem to be disaster,
The things that hurt . . .
So close I cannot hear
Your voice in this dim void.

And so I wait,
As a blind, deaf man awaits
The mere sensation of sound

(The rushing of the wind
Or the rumble of
Wild horses' hooves
On distant ground),
So *I* wait to sense the signs of
You . . .
The breeze of Your breath
Or the far vibrations
Of Your footsteps.

And Lo! Like a surging,
Silent song I feel
The sudden pulse of Your presence
In my soul . . .
As close
As clearly
As the heartbeat
In my breast!

O Lord! Until the veil is lifted,
Until I know
Even as I am known,
It is enough!

Postscript

I laid me down, Lord,
But I couldn't sleep . . .
At least not until
I tell You how
Grateful I am!
You know what You
Did for me today . . .
You know how
Much it mattered!
But I couldn't let
The day be done
Until I wrote this
One last line . . .

PRAISE BE!